contents

Please note that Australian cup and
spoon measurements are metric.
A conversion chart appears on page 62.

fruity white chocolate bars

⅔ cup (90g) slivered almonds
1¼ cups (210g) brazil nuts, coarsely chopped
1½ cups (135g) desiccated coconut
1 cup (150g) chopped dried apricots
1 cup (150g) dried currants
¼ cup (35g) plain flour
250g white Choc Melts, melted
½ cup (160g) apricot jam
½ cup (180g) honey

Preheat oven to moderately slow.
Lightly grease 19cm x 29cm rectangular
slice pan; cover base with baking paper.
Combine nuts, coconut, fruit and flour in large
bowl. Stir in combined hot chocolate, sieved jam
and honey. Spread evenly into prepared pan;
bake in moderately slow oven for 45 minutes.
Cool in pan before cutting into pieces. Dust with
icing sugar, if desired.

makes about 16
tip This recipe can be made a week ahead and
kept, covered, in the refrigerator; it can also be
frozen for up to two months.

fudgy choc nut brownies

125g butter, chopped
90g dark eating chocolate, chopped coarsely
90g milk eating chocolate, chopped coarsely
½ cup (110g) firmly packed brown sugar
2 tablespoons honey
2 eggs, beaten lightly
1 cup (150g) plain flour
⅔ cup (100g) macadamia nuts, chopped coarsely

Preheat oven to moderate. Grease deep 19cm-square cake pan; cover base with baking paper.
Combine butter and chocolate in medium saucepan; stir over low heat until melted. Remove from heat; stir in sugar and honey. Stir in egg, then sifted flour and nuts; pour mixture into prepared pan.
Bake in moderate oven about 30 minutes or until firm. Cool in pan; cut into squares when cold.

makes about 12
tip This recipe can be made a week ahead and kept, covered, in the refrigerator.

no-bake chocolate slice

200g packet white marshmallows
1 tablespoon water
90g butter, chopped
200g dark eating chocolate, chopped coarsely
125g plain sweet biscuits, chopped coarsely
½ cup (125g) halved glacé cherries
½ cup (75g) roasted hazelnuts
½ cup (50g) walnuts
200g dark eating chocolate, melted, extra
60g butter, melted, extra

Grease two 8cm x 25cm bar pans; line bases and sides with baking paper, extending 2cm above long edges of pans.

Combine marshmallows, the water and butter in medium saucepan. Stir constantly over low heat until marshmallows are melted. Remove pan from heat. Add chocolate; stir until melted.

Add biscuits, cherries and nuts to marshmallow mixture; stir gently until ingredients are combined. Spread mixture evenly into prepared pans (do not crush biscuits). Cover; refrigerate 1 hour.

Combine extra chocolate and extra butter; spread mixture evenly over slices. Refrigerate 1 hour or until firm. Remove slices from pans. Peel away paper; cut each into 12 pieces.

makes about 24

tips This recipe can be made a week ahead and kept, covered, in the refrigerator.
Pecans can be used instead of walnuts, if preferred.

no-bowl choc-bit slice

90g butter, melted
1 cup (100g) plain sweet biscuit crumbs
1½ cups (285g) dark Choc Bits
1 cup (70g) shredded coconut
1 cup (140g) crushed mixed nuts
395g can sweetened condensed milk

Preheat oven to moderate. Grease 23cm-square
slab pan; line base and sides with baking paper.
Pour butter into prepared pan; sprinkle evenly
with biscuit crumbs, Choc Bits, coconut and nuts.
Drizzle with condensed milk.
Bake in moderate oven about 30 minutes.
Cool in pan before cutting into pieces.

makes about 18
tip This recipe can be made a week ahead and
kept, covered, in the refrigerator.

chocolate cornflake slice

¾ cup (45g) shredded coconut
¾ cup (165g) firmly packed brown sugar
1½ cups (225g) self-raising flour
2 cups (80g) cornflakes
½ cup (95g) dark Choc Bits
185g butter, melted, cooled
1 egg, beaten lightly
125g dark eating chocolate, melted

Preheat oven to moderate. Grease 20cm x 30cm lamington pan; line base and two long sides with baking paper, extending paper 2cm above edge of pan.
Combine coconut, sugar, sifted flour, cornflakes and Choc Bits in large bowl. Stir in combined butter and egg. Press mixture into base of prepared pan.
Bake in moderate oven about 20 minutes or until browned lightly; stand 5 minutes before turning slice onto wire rack to cool.
Cut slice into pieces. Place melted chocolate into a small piping bag and drizzle over each piece.

makes about 25
tips If you do not have a small piping bag, place the melted chocolate in a small plastic sandwich bag and snip off one corner. If the chocolate starts to set while you are piping, microwave for about 5 seconds on HIGH (100%) power.
This recipe can be made a week ahead; store in an airtight container.

chocolate rum and raisin slice

125g butter, chopped
200g dark eating chocolate, chopped
½ cup (110g) caster sugar
1 cup (170g) coarsely chopped raisins
2 eggs, beaten lightly
1½ cups (225g) plain flour
1 tablespoon dark rum

Preheat oven to moderately slow. Grease
20cm x 30cm lamington pan.
Combine butter, chocolate, sugar and raisins
in medium saucepan; stir over low heat until
chocolate is melted. Cool to room temperature.
Stir in remaining ingredients, mix well; spread
mixture into prepared pan.
Bake in moderately slow oven about 30 minutes
or until just firm; cool in pan. Serve dusted with
sifted icing sugar, if desired.

makes about 15
tip This recipe can be made a week ahead;
store in an airtight container.

maple caramel slice

200g packet plain un-iced chocolate biscuits,
   crushed finely
½ cup (45g) desiccated coconut
200g butter, melted
100g dark eating chocolate, melted
2 teaspoons vegetable oil
maple caramel
395g can sweetened condensed milk
60g butter
2 tablespoons maple-flavoured syrup

Grease 19cm x 29cm rectangular slice pan;
line base and two long sides with baking paper,
extending paper 2cm above edge of pan.
Combine biscuit crumbs, coconut and butter
in large bowl; press over base of prepared pan.
Cover; refrigerate until firm. Spread hot maple
caramel over crumb layer, cover; refrigerate
until firm. Spread combined chocolate and
oil over slice; leave to set.
Maple caramel Combine ingredients in medium
saucepan; whisk over heat until butter melts.
Simmer, whisking constantly, about 8 minutes or
until mixture thickens and is dark golden brown.

makes about 24
tip This recipe can be made a week ahead and
kept, covered, in the refrigerator.

caramel coconut slice

½ cup (75g) plain flour
½ cup (75g) self-raising flour
½ cup (45g) desiccated coconut
½ cup (110g) caster sugar
100g butter, melted
caramel filling
395g can sweetened condensed milk
2 tablespoons golden syrup
¼ cup (55g) firmly packed brown sugar
60g butter, melted
coconut topping
4 eggs, beaten lightly
⅔ cup (150g) caster sugar
4 cups (360g) desiccated coconut

Preheat oven to moderate.
Grease 25cm x 30cm swiss roll pan.
Sift flours into medium bowl, stir in coconut,
sugar and butter; press mixture evenly over
base of prepared pan. Bake in moderate oven
about 10 minutes or until lightly browned; cool.
Spread caramel filling evenly over base; sprinkle
with coconut topping. Bake in moderate oven
about 25 minutes or until topping is lightly
browned; cool in pan.
Caramel filling Combine ingredients
in bowl; mix well.
Coconut topping Combine ingredients
in bowl; mix well.

makes about 12
tip This recipe can be made a week ahead;
store in an airtight container.

coffee malt surprise slice

200g packet Coffee Eclairs
1 tablespoon cream
1 cup (35g) Rice Bubbles
100g packet marshmallows, chopped coarsely
165g packet Maltesers

Grease 8cm x 25cm bar cake pan; line base
and two short sides with baking paper.
Combine Eclairs and cream in medium
heavy-based saucepan; stir over low heat until
smooth. Remove from heat, stir in Rice Bubbles
and marshmallows; quickly stir in Maltesers.
Press mixture lightly into prepared pan; refrigerate
until set. Cut into slices with a serrated knife.

makes about 15
tip This recipe can be made a week ahead
and kept, covered, in the refrigerator.

fruit chews

⅓ cup (75g) firmly packed brown sugar
90g butter
1¼ cups (185g) plain flour
1 egg yolk
topping
2 eggs
1 cup (220g) firmly packed brown sugar
⅓ cup (50g) self-raising flour
½ cup (85g) raisins
¾ cup (120g) sultanas
1¼ cups (185g) roasted unsalted peanuts
1 cup (90g) desiccated coconut

Preheat oven to moderate. Grease
20cm x 30cm lamington pan; line base and
two long sides with baking paper, extending
paper 2cm above edge of pan.
Combine sugar and butter in medium saucepan;
stir over medium heat until butter is melted. Stir in
sifted flour and egg yolk. Press mixture over base
of prepared pan. Bake in moderate oven about
10 minutes or until browned lightly; cool.
Spread topping over cold base; bake in moderate
oven about 30 minutes or until browned lightly.
Cool in pan before cutting into pieces.
Topping Beat eggs and sugar in small bowl with
electric mixer until changed to a lighter colour and
thickened slightly; fold in sifted flour. Transfer mixture
to large bowl; stir in remaining ingredients.

makes about 18
tip This recipe can be made a week ahead;
store in an airtight container.

nut cluster bars

1 cup (100g) plain sweet biscuit crumbs
60g butter, melted
½ cup (80g) blanched almonds, chopped coarsely
⅓ cup (50g) shelled pistachios, chopped coarsely
¼ cup (35g) macadamias, chopped coarsely
3 glacé pineapple rings (85g), chopped coarsely
200g white Choc Melts, melted
185g butter, melted, extra
200g dark eating chocolate, melted

Grease 19cm x 29cm rectangular slice pan;
line base and two long sides with baking paper,
extending paper 2cm above edge of pan.
Combine crumbs and butter in medium bowl,
press evenly over base of prepared pan; refrigerate.
Combine nuts and pineapple in medium bowl,
mix well; divide nut mixture between two bowls.
Combine white Melts with ⅔ of the extra butter,
stir into one bowl of nut mixture; pour over biscuit
base, refrigerate until set.
Stir remaining butter and dark chocolate into
remaining bowl of nut mixture, spread over white
chocolate layer; cover, refrigerate until set.

makes about 12
tip This recipe can be made a week ahead
and kept, covered, in the refrigerator.

pepita and sesame slice

90g butter
1 teaspoon grated lemon rind
2 tablespoons caster sugar
1 egg
⅔ cup (100g) white plain flour
½ cup (80g) wholemeal plain flour
½ cup (80g) unsalted pepitas (pumpkin seed kernels),
    chopped coarsely
¼ cup (80g) apricot jam
2 tablespoons sesame seeds, toasted

Preheat oven to moderately hot. Grease
23cm-square slab pan; line base and two
opposite sides with baking paper, extending
paper 2cm above edge of pan.
Beat butter, rind, sugar and egg in small bowl with
electric mixer until light and fluffy. Stir in sifted flours
and pepitas; press mixture evenly into prepared pan.
Spread base with jam; sprinkle with seeds.
Bake in moderately hot oven about 20 minutes
or until lightly browned; cool slice in pan.

makes about 16
tip This recipe can be made a week ahead;
store in an airtight container.

chewy peanut butter bars

60g butter, chopped
¼ cup (90g) honey
½ cup (110g) firmly packed brown sugar
⅓ cup (95g) smooth peanut butter
2 tablespoons marmalade
1 cup (90g) rolled oats
1½ cups (50g) Rice Bubbles
½ cup (35g) shredded coconut
½ cup (75g) mixed dried fruit
¼ cup (55g) finely chopped glacé pineapple

Grease 23cm-square slab pan.
Combine butter, honey, sugar, peanut butter and marmalade in large saucepan; stir over low heat, without boiling, until sugar is dissolved. Bring to a boil; remove from heat. Stir in remaining ingredients; mix well.
Press mixture firmly into prepared pan; refrigerate until firm.

makes about 24
tip This recipe can be made a week ahead and kept, covered, in the refrigerator.

lemon cream cheese slice

2 x 150g packets coconut macaroons, crushed
140g butter, melted
2 tablespoons honey
filling
3 teaspoons powdered gelatine
¼ cup (60ml) water
500g packaged cream cheese, softened, chopped
280g jar lemon butter
½ cup (120g) sour cream

Grease 20cm x 30cm lamington pan; line base
and two long sides with baking paper, extending
paper 2cm above edge of pan.

Combine macaroons, butter and honey in medium
bowl; mix well. Press into prepared pan, roughen
surface using a fork. Pour filling over macaroon base;
refrigerate until firm.

Filling Sprinkle gelatine over the water in cup.
Stand in small pan of simmering water; stir until
dissolved. Beat cheese in medium bowl with
electric mixer until smooth. Add gelatine mixture
and remaining ingredients; beat until smooth.

makes about 10

tip This recipe can be made three days ahead
and kept, covered, in the refrigerator.

lemon coconut slice

90g butter, chopped
⅔ cup (150g) caster sugar
1 egg
¼ cup (35g) self-raising flour
¾ cup (110g) plain flour
280g jar lemon butter
topping
2 eggs, beaten lightly
⅓ cup (75g) caster sugar
2 cups (180g) desiccated coconut

Preheat oven to moderate. Grease 20cm x 30cm
lamington pan.
Beat butter, sugar and egg in small bowl with
electric mixer until light and fluffy; stir in combined
sifted flours. With lightly floured hands, press mixture
evenly over base of prepared pan. Place pan in
freezer for 15 minutes, then bake in moderate oven
about 15 minutes or until browned lightly; cool.
Meanwhile, place lemon butter in small bowl;
whisk until smooth. Spread lemon butter over
cold base, then sprinkle with topping.
Bake in moderate oven about 35 minutes or
until browned; cool slice in pan before cutting.
Topping Combine ingredients in medium
bowl; mix well.

makes about 24
tip This recipe can be made a week ahead;
store in an airtight container.

fruit coconut bubble slice

2 cups (140g) shredded coconut
3 cups (105g) Rice Bubbles
⅔ cup (50g) All-Bran
1 cup (250g) coarsely chopped glacé apricots
½ cup (115g) coarsely chopped glacé pineapple
1 cup (125g) coarsely chopped pecans
125g butter
½ cup (125ml) coconut cream
½ cup (180g) honey
⅓ cup (75g) raw sugar

Grease 20cm x 30cm lamington pan.
Combine coconut, Rice Bubbles, All-Bran, fruit and nuts in large bowl.
Combine butter, coconut cream, honey and sugar in small saucepan; stir over low heat, without boiling, until butter is melted and sugar dissolved.
Bring to a boil; simmer, uncovered, without stirring, about 5 minutes or until mixture resembles a thick syrup. Stir hot mixture into dry ingredients; mix well. Press into prepared pan; refrigerate until firm.

makes about 28
tips This recipe can be made a week ahead and kept, covered, in the refrigerator.
Walnuts can be used instead of pecans, if preferred.

cashew ginger squares

125g butter
¼ cup (55g) caster sugar
1 cup (150g) self-raising flour
1 teaspoon ground ginger
topping
½ cup (80g) icing sugar mixture
60g butter
2 tablespoons golden syrup
1 cup (150g) unsalted roasted cashews,
    chopped coarsely
¼ cup (50g) finely chopped glacé ginger

Preheat oven to moderate. Grease 20cm x 30cm
lamington pan; line base and two long sides with baking
paper, extending paper 2cm above edge of pan.
Beat butter and sugar in small bowl with electric mixer
until light and fluffy; stir in sifted flour and ginger.
Spread mixture evenly over base of prepared pan.
Bake in moderate oven about 20 minutes or until
lightly browned; cool in pan.
Spread hot topping evenly over cold base; cool.
Topping Combine sifted icing sugar, butter and syrup
in small saucepan; stir over heat until butter is melted.
Stir in nuts and ginger.

makes about 12
tip This recipe can be made a week ahead and kept,
covered, in the refrigerator.

date and banana slice

½ cup (80g) seeded,
  coarsely chopped
  dried dates
¼ cup (60ml) water
1 tablespoon honey
90g butter
¾ cup (165g) raw sugar
1 cup (150g)
  self-raising flour
¼ cup (35g) plain flour
½ teaspoon
  ground nutmeg
¾ cup (45g)
  unprocessed bran
⅓ cup mashed banana
ground nutmeg, extra
lemon icing
2½ cups (400g) icing
  sugar mixture
30g softened butter
2 tablespoons
  lemon juice
1 tablespoon water,
  approximately

Preheat oven to moderate. Grease 25cm x 30cm swiss roll pan.

Combine dates, the water and honey in small saucepan; bring to a boil. Simmer, uncovered, for 2 minutes or until slightly thickened; cool.

Beat butter and sugar in small bowl with electric mixer until combined. Stir in sifted flours and nutmeg, date mixture, bran and banana. Spread mixture evenly over base of prepared pan.

Bake in moderate oven about 30 minutes or until firm; stand 20 minutes. Spread with lemon icing; sprinkle with a little extra nutmeg.

Lemon icing Sift icing sugar into small heatproof bowl; stir in butter and juice, and enough water to give a stiff paste. Stir over pan of simmering water until spreadable.

makes about 25
tips Any type of bran can be used in this recipe. This recipe can be made a week ahead; store in an airtight container.

fruity almond pistachio slice

¾ cup (180ml) sweetened condensed milk
125g butter, chopped
2 teaspoons grated lemon rind
1½ cups (150g) plain sweet biscuit crumbs
½ cup (125g) coarsely chopped red glacé cherries
½ cup (150g) coarsely chopped glacé figs
½ cup (125g) coarsely chopped glacé peaches
⅓ cup (55g) coarsely chopped
    almond kernels, toasted
⅓ cup (50g) coarsely chopped pistachios, toasted
¾ cup (65g) desiccated coconut
100g dark eating chocolate, melted
60g butter, melted, extra
1 tablespoon coarsely chopped
    almond kernels, extra
1 tablespoon coarsely chopped pistachios, extra

Grease 19cm x 29cm rectangular slice pan; line base and two opposite sides with baking paper.
Combine condensed milk, butter and rind in medium saucepan; stir over heat until butter is melted. Add biscuit crumbs, fruit, nuts and coconut; mix well.
Press mixture evenly over base of prepared pan. Spread with combined chocolate and extra butter, sprinkle with extra nuts; refrigerate until set.

makes about 24
tip This recipe can be made a week ahead and kept, covered, in the refrigerator.

marmalade almond coconut squares

125g butter, chopped
1 teaspoon almond essence
¼ cup (55g) caster sugar
1 cup (150g) plain flour
¼ cup (20g) desiccated coconut
⅓ cup (15g) flaked coconut
¼ cup (85g) marmalade, warmed
topping
90g butter, chopped
2 teaspoons grated orange rind
⅓ cup (75g) caster sugar
2 eggs
1 cup (90g) desiccated coconut
1 cup (125g) almond meal

Preheat oven to moderately hot. Grease
19cm x 29cm rectangular slice pan.
Beat butter, essence and sugar in small bowl with
electric mixer until smooth. Stir in flour and desiccated
coconut; press into prepared pan. Bake in moderately
hot oven about 15 minutes or until browned.
Reduce oven temperature to moderate. Spread
hot slice with topping; sprinkle with flaked coconut.
Bake in moderate oven about 20 minutes or until
firm. Brush hot slice with marmalade; cool in pan.
Topping Beat butter, rind and sugar in small bowl
with electric mixer until smooth; add eggs, beat until
combined (mixture will look curdled at this stage).
Stir in coconut and almond meal.

makes about 18
tip This recipe can be made a week ahead
and kept, covered, in the refrigerator.

passionfruit custard slice

You will need about 4 passionfruit for this recipe.

1 cup (150g) plain flour
125g butter, chopped
2 tablespoons icing sugar mixture
2 teaspoons powdered gelatine
⅓ cup (80ml) lemon juice
395g can sweetened condensed milk
⅓ cup (40g) custard powder
1 cup (220g) caster sugar
2 tablespoons milk
1½ cups (375ml) water
20g butter, extra
2 tablespoons lemon juice, extra
⅓ cup (80ml) passionfruit pulp

Preheat oven to moderate. Grease 20cm x 30cm lamington pan; line base and two long sides with baking paper, extending paper 2cm above edge of pan.

Process flour, butter and icing sugar until combined. Press over base of prepared pan; bake in moderate oven about 20 minutes. Cool in pan.

Sprinkle gelatine over juice in cup; stand in small pan of simmering water, stir until dissolved. Beat gelatine mixture and condensed milk in small bowl with electric mixer about 10 minutes or until mixture thickens. Pour over base.

Blend custard powder and caster sugar with milk and the water in small saucepan; cook, stirring, over heat until mixture boils and thickens. Remove from heat, stir in extra butter; cover, stand 10 minutes. Stir in extra juice and passionfruit pulp. Pour over gelatine layer in pan. Refrigerate until set, before cutting.

makes about 8
tip This recipe can be made three days ahead and kept, covered, in the refrigerator.

hazelnut caramel slice

200g butter, chopped
½ cup (50g) cocoa
  powder
2 cups (440g) firmly
  packed brown sugar
1 teaspoon vanilla extract
2 eggs, beaten lightly
1½ cups (225g)
  plain flour
200g dark eating
  chocolate, melted,
  cooled
1 tablespoon vegetable oil
caramel filling
180g butter, chopped
½ cup (110g) caster sugar
2 tablespoons
  golden syrup
¾ cup (180ml) sweetened
  condensed milk
1¼ cups (175g) whole
  hazelnuts, roasted

Preheat oven to moderately slow. Grease 20cm x 30cm lamington pan; line base and two long sides with baking paper.

Combine butter and cocoa powder in medium saucepan; stir over low heat until smooth. Add sugar; stir until dissolved. Remove from heat; add vanilla, egg and sifted flour, mix well. Spread mixture into prepared pan, bake in moderately slow oven for 20 minutes; cool.

Quickly spread caramel filling evenly over base; refrigerate at least 30 minutes or until firm. Combine chocolate and oil in small bowl, spread over caramel filling; refrigerate until set.

Caramel filling Combine butter, sugar, syrup and condensed milk in medium saucepan; stir over low heat until butter is melted. Increase heat to medium and simmer, stirring, about 10 minutes or until mixture is a dark caramel colour. Remove from heat; stir in hazelnuts.

makes about 20
tip This recipe can be made two days ahead and kept, covered, in the refrigerator.

date squares

1¼ cups (185g) plain flour
1¼ cups (200g) wholemeal plain flour
200g butter, chopped
½ cup (110g) caster sugar
1 egg, beaten lightly
1 tablespoon water, approximately
1 tablespoon milk
1 tablespoon raw sugar
2 teaspoons caster sugar, extra
apple date filling
1 medium apple (150g), peeled, sliced finely
1½ cups (225g) seeded dried dates,
   chopped coarsely
½ cup (125ml) water

Preheat oven to moderately hot. Grease 25cm x 30cm
swiss roll pan; line base and two long sides with baking
paper, extending paper 2cm above edge of pan.
Sift flours into large bowl; rub in butter, stir in caster
sugar. Add egg and enough water to mix to a firm
dough. Knead on floured surface until smooth, cover;
refrigerate 30 minutes.
Roll out half of the dough until large enough to cover
base of prepared pan; spread with cold apple date
filling. Roll out remaining dough until large enough to
cover filling; brush with milk, sprinkle with raw sugar.
Bake in moderately hot oven about 25 minutes; cool
in pan before cutting. Sprinkle with extra caster sugar.
Apple date filling Combine ingredients in small
saucepan; simmer, covered, about 5 minutes or until
mixture is pulpy. Blend or process until smooth; cool.

makes about 16
tip This recipe can be made a week ahead;
store in an airtight container.

luscious choc macadamia squares

200g packet plain un-iced chocolate biscuits,
    crushed finely
185g butter, melted
2 x 395g cans sweetened condensed milk
50g butter
2 tablespoons golden syrup
1 cup (150g) macadamias, toasted, chopped coarsely
200g dark eating chocolate, melted
50g butter, melted, extra

Grease 20cm x 30cm lamington pan; line base
and two long sides with baking paper, extending
paper 2cm above edge of pan.
Combine biscuit crumbs and butter in medium
bowl; press over base of prepared pan. Cover;
refrigerate until firm.
Combine condensed milk, butter and syrup in
medium saucepan; whisk over heat until butter melts.
Simmer, whisking constantly, about 8 minutes or until
mixture thickens and is dark golden brown. Stir in nuts;
spread over crumb layer. Cover; refrigerate until firm.
Spread combined chocolate and extra butter over
caramel layer; refrigerate until set.

makes about 20
tip This recipe can be made a week ahead and
kept, covered, in the refrigerator.

apricot muesli bars

125g butter, chopped
½ cup (110g) firmly packed brown sugar
1 tablespoon honey
2¼ cups (200g) rolled oats
¼ cup (40g) sunflower kernels
¼ cup (20g) desiccated coconut
½ teaspoon ground cinnamon
½ cup (75g) chopped dried apricots
2 tablespoons dark Choc Bits

Preheat oven to moderately slow.
Grease 20cm x 30cm lamington pan.
Combine butter, sugar and honey in
medium saucepan; stir over low heat
until sugar is dissolved.
Transfer butter mixture to medium bowl;
stir in oats, sunflower kernels, coconut,
cinnamon and apricots. Press mixture into
prepared pan; sprinkle with Choc Bits.
Bake in moderately slow oven about
30 minutes or until browned lightly. Cut into
pieces while still warm; cool in pan.

makes about 8
tip This recipe can be made a week ahead
and kept, covered, in the refrigerator.

almond honey squares

1 cup (150g) plain flour
½ teaspoon ground nutmeg
½ cup (60g) almond meal
½ cup (110g) firmly packed brown sugar
90g butter, melted
1½ cups (210g) slivered almonds
topping
3 eggs, beaten lightly
¼ cup (55g) firmly packed brown sugar
¼ cup (90g) honey
100g milk Choc Melts, melted

Preheat oven to moderate. Grease
20cm x 30cm lamington pan.
Combine sifted flour, nutmeg, almond meal, sugar
and butter in medium bowl. Press mixture evenly
over base of prepared pan. Bake in moderate oven
about 12 minutes or until lightly browned; cool.
Reduce oven temperature to moderately slow.
Pour topping over base; sprinkle with slivered
almonds. Bake in moderately slow oven about
40 minutes or until topping is set. Cool in pan;
refrigerate for several hours before cutting.
Topping Combine egg, sugar and honey in
medium bowl; stir in Melts.

makes about 20
tip This recipe can be made a week ahead
and kept, covered, in the refrigerator.

apricot crumble slice

90g butter, melted
1 cup (150g) plain flour
⅓ cup (75g) caster sugar
filling
1⅔ cups (250g) finely chopped dried apricots
1 cup (250ml) water
¼ cup (55g) caster sugar
coconut topping
90g butter, melted
⅓ cup (30g) desiccated coconut
¼ cup (15g) shredded coconut
½ cup (75g) plain flour
½ cup (110g) firmly packed brown sugar

Preheat oven to moderate. Grease
19cm x 29cm rectangular slice pan.
Combine butter, flour and sugar in small bowl;
press mixture over base of prepared pan.
Bake in moderate oven about 20 minutes or
until browned. Spread hot filling over hot base;
sprinkle with coconut topping.
Bake in moderate oven about 20 minutes or
until browned; cool in pan.
Filling Combine apricots, the water and sugar
in medium saucepan; simmer, uncovered, about
10 minutes or until thick, stirring occasionally.
Coconut topping Combine ingredients in
medium bowl; mix well.

makes about 12
tip This recipe can be made a week ahead;
store in an airtight container.

tangy lemon squares

125g butter
¼ cup (40g) icing sugar mixture
1¼ cups (185g) plain flour
3 eggs
1 cup (220g) caster sugar
2 teaspoons grated lemon rind
½ cup (125ml) lemon juice

Preheat oven to moderate. Grease 23cm-square slab pan; line base and two opposite sides of pan with baking paper.

Beat butter and icing sugar in small bowl with electric mixer until smooth. Stir in 1 cup (150g) of the flour. Press mixture over base of prepared pan. Bake in moderate oven about 15 minutes or until browned lightly.

Place eggs, caster sugar, remaining flour, rind and juice in medium bowl; whisk until combined. Pour egg mixture over hot base. Bake in moderate oven about 20 minutes or until firm. Cool in pan on a wire rack.

Lift slice from pan and cut into pieces. Dust with extra sifted icing sugar, if desired.

makes about 16
tip This recipe can be made three days ahead and kept, covered, in the refrigerator.

orange poppyseed shortbread bars

200g softened butter, chopped
2 teaspoons grated orange rind
½ cup (80g) icing sugar mixture
2 cups (300g) plain flour
1 tablespoon poppyseeds
1 tablespoon orange juice

Preheat oven to moderately slow.
Grease 20cm x 30cm lamington pan.
Beat butter, rind and sugar in medium
bowl with electric mixer until light and fluffy.
Stir in flour, seeds and juice. Press mixture
together firmly. Press into prepared pan;
mark into finger lengths.
Bake in moderately slow oven about
35 minutes or until lightly browned. Cut
into finger lengths in pan; cool in pan.

makes about 24
tip This recipe can be made a week ahead;
store in an airtight container.

glossary

all-bran a low-fat, high-fibre breakfast cereal based on wheat bran.

almond flat, pointy-ended nuts with pitted brown shell enclosing a creamy white kernel covered by brown skin.

blanched: almond kernel with brown skin removed.

essence: also known as extract.

meal: also known as ground almonds; nuts are powdered to a coarse flour texture.

slivered: small lengthways-cut almond pieces.

apricot, glacé apricot cooked in heavy sugar syrup, then dried.

biscuits also known as cookies.

bran, unprocessed made from outer layer of a cereal, most often the husks of wheat, rice or oats.

brazil nut triangular nut with a hard shell; has white flesh encased with a brown skin.

butter use salted or unsalted (sweet) butter; 125g is equal to one stick of butter.

cherries, glacé cherries cooked in heavy sugar syrup, then dried.

chocolate

choc bits: also known as choc chips and chocolate morsels; available in milk, white and dark chocolate.

choc melts: discs of compounded, dark, milk or white chocolate ideal for melting or moulding.

dark eating: made of cocoa liquor, cocoa butter and sugar.

milk eating: used primarily for eating rather than cooking.

cinnamon dried inner bark of the shoots of the cinnamon tree; available in stick or ground form.

cocoa powder also known as cocoa; dried, unsweetened cocoa beans that have been roasted then ground.

coconut

cream: obtained commercially from the first pressing of the coconut flesh, without the addition of water; the second pressing (less rich) is sold as the milk. Available in cans and cartons at supermarkets.

desiccated: finely shredded, dried coconut.

flaked: dried, flaked coconut.

macaroons: small biscuit (cookie) made with coconut.

shredded: thin strips of dried coconut.

cornflakes crisp flakes of corn.

coffee eclairs coffee-flavoured sweet made with glucose, sugar, condensed milk, chocolate, oil and coffee extract.

cream cheese commonly known as Philadelphia or Philly, a soft cow-milk cheese with a fat content of at least 33%. Sold at supermarkets in bulk and packaged.

currants, dried tiny, almost black raisins, so-named after a grape variety that originated in Corinth, Greece.

custard powder packaged vanilla mixture, used to make pouring custard.

dates, dried dried, oval-shaped fruit of the date palm.

fig, glacé fig cooked in heavy sugar syrup, then dried.

flour

plain: an all-purpose flour, made from wheat.

self-raising: plain flour sifted with baking powder in the proportion of 1 cup flour to 2 teaspoons baking powder.

wholemeal plain: also known as all-purpose wholewheat flour; has no baking powder added.

gelatine we used powdered gelatine. Also available in sheet form, known as leaf gelatine.

ginger, glacé ginger cooked in heavy sugar syrup, then dried.

golden syrup a by-product of refined sugarcane; pure maple syrup or honey can be substituted.

hazelnut also known as filberts; plump, grape-sized, sweet nut with brown inedible skin that is removed by rubbing heated nuts together vigorously in a tea towel.

jam also known as preserve or conserve.

lamington pan 20cm x 30cm cake pan, 3cm deep.

lemon butter also known as lemon curd, lemon cheese or lemon spread.

macadamia rich, buttery nut native to Australia; due to high oil content, store in refrigerator.

maltesers chocolates with crisp, light honeycomb centres; made from chocolate, glucose syrup, malt extract, milk powder, flour and sugar.

maple-flavoured syrup made from sugar cane; also known as golden or pancake syrup. It is not a substitute for pure maple syrup.

marmalade a preserve, usually based on citrus fruit.

marshmallow pink and white; made from sugar, glucose, gelatine and cornflour.

nutmeg the dried nut of an evergreen tree native to Indonesia; it is available in ground form, or you can grate your own with a fine grater.

nuts, crushed mixed packaged crushed nuts, available from supermarkets.

peach, glacé peach cooked in heavy sugar syrup, then dried.

peanut butter peanuts ground to a paste; available in crunchy and smooth varieties.

pecan a golden-brown, rich, buttery nut.

pepitas dried pumpkin seeds.

pineapple, glacé pineapple cooked in heavy sugar syrup, then dried.

pistachio pale green nut inside hard off-white shells. To peel, soak shelled nuts in boiling water for about 5 minutes; drain, then pat dry. Rub skins with cloth to peel.

poppyseeds tiny black seeds with a pungent flavour; store in an airtight container in a cool place or freezer.

raisins dried sweet grapes.

rice bubbles puffed rice breakfast cereal.

rolled oats oat groats (husked oats); steam-softened, flattened with rollers, dried and packaged for consumption as a cereal product.

rum, dark we prefer to use an underproof rum (not overproof) for a more subtle flavour.

sesame seeds black and white are the most common of this small oval seed, however, there are red and brown varieties, also. To toast: spread seeds evenly on oven tray, toast in moderate oven briefly.

sour cream a thick, commercially cultured soured cream with a minimum fat content of 35%.

sugar we used coarse, granulated table sugar, also known as crystal sugar, unless otherwise specified.

caster: also known as superfine or finely granulated table sugar.

brown: an extremely soft, fine granulated sugar retaining molasses for its characteristic colour and flavour.

icing sugar mixture: also known as confectioners' sugar or powdered sugar; granulated sugar crushed together with a small amount (about 3%) cornflour added.

raw: natural brown granulated sugar.

sultanas dried grapes, also known as golden raisins.

sunflower kernels from dried husked sunflower seeds.

sweetened condensed milk condensed milk from which 60% of the water has been removed; the remaining milk is then sweetened with sugar.

vanilla extract also known as vanilla essence.

vegetable oil any of a number of oils sourced from plants rather than animal fats.

conversion chart

MEASURES

One Australian metric measuring cup holds approximately 250ml, one Australian metric tablespoon holds 20ml, one Australian metric teaspoon holds 5ml.

The difference between one country's measuring cups and another's is within a two- or three-teaspoon variance, and will not affect your cooking results. North America, New Zealand and the United Kingdom use a 15ml tablespoon.

All cup and spoon measurements are level. The most accurate way of measuring dry ingredients is to weigh them. When measuring liquids, use a clear glass or plastic jug with the metric markings.

We use large eggs with an average weight of 60g.

DRY MEASURES

METRIC	IMPERIAL
15g	½oz
30g	1oz
60g	2oz
90g	3oz
125g	4oz (¼lb)
155g	5oz
185g	6oz
220g	7oz
250g	8oz (½lb)
280g	9oz
315g	10oz
345g	11oz
375g	12oz (¾lb)
410g	13oz
440g	14oz
470g	15oz
500g	16oz (1lb)
750g	24oz (1½lb)
1kg	32oz (2lb)

LIQUID MEASURES

METRIC	IMPERIAL
30ml	1 fluid oz
60ml	2 fluid oz
100ml	3 fluid oz
125ml	4 fluid oz
150ml	5 fluid oz (¼ pint/1 gill)
190ml	6 fluid oz
250ml	8 fluid oz
300ml	10 fluid oz (½ pint)
500ml	16 fluid oz
600ml	20 fluid oz (1 pint)
1000ml (1 litre)	1¾ pints

LENGTH MEASURES

METRIC	IMPERIAL
3mm	⅛in
6mm	¼in
1cm	½in
2cm	¾in
2.5cm	1in
5cm	2in
6cm	2½in
8cm	3in
10cm	4in
13cm	5in
15cm	6in
18cm	7in
20cm	8in
23cm	9in
25cm	10in
28cm	11in
30cm	12in (1ft)

OVEN TEMPERATURES

These oven temperatures are only a guide for conventional ovens.
For fan-forced ovens, check the manufacturer's manual.

	°C (CELSIUS)	°F (FAHRENHEIT)	GAS MARK
Very slow	120	250	½
Slow	150	275 – 300	1 – 2
Moderately slow	160	325	3
Moderate	180	350 – 375	4 – 5
Moderately hot	200	400	6
Hot	220	425 – 450	7 – 8
Very hot	240	475	9

index

Are you missing some of the world's favourite cookbooks?

The Australian Women's Weekly cookbooks are available from bookshops, cookshops, supermarkets and other stores all over the world. You can also buy direct from the publisher, using the order form below.

MINI SERIES £3.50 190x138MM 64 PAGES

TITLE	QTY	TITLE	QTY	TITLE	QTY
4 Fast Ingredients		Healthy Everyday Food 4 Kids		Simple Slices	
4 Kids to Cook		Ice-creams & Sorbets		Simply Seafood	
15-minute Feasts		Indian Cooking		Soup plus	
50 Fast Chicken Fillets		Italian Favourites		Spanish Favourites	
50 Fast Desserts		Indonesian Favourites		Stir-fries	
Biscuits, Brownies & Bisottti		Jams & Jellies		Stir-fry Favourites	
Bites		Japanese Favourites		Summer Salads	
Bowl Food		Kebabs & Skewers		Tagines & Couscous	
Burgers, Rösti & Fritters		Kids Party Food		Tapas, Antipasto & Mezze	
Cafe Cakes		Lebanese Cooking		Tarts	
Cafe Food		Low-Fat Delicious		Tex-Mex	
Casseroles & Curries		Low Fat Fast		Thai Favourites	
Char-grills & Barbecues		Malaysian Favourites		The Fast Egg	
Cheesecakes, Pavlova & Trifles		Mince Favourites		The Young Chef	
Chinese Favourites		Muffins		Vegetarian	
Chocolate Cakes		Noodles & Stir-fries		Vegie Main Meals	
Crumbles & Bakes		Old-Fashioned Desserts		Vietnamese Favourites	
Cupcakes & Cookies		Outdoor Eating			
Dips & Dippers		Packed Lunch			
Dried Fruit & Nuts		Party Food			
Drinks		Pickles and Chutneys			
Easy Pies & Pastries		Pasta			
Fast Fillets		Potatoes		TOTAL COST £	
Fishcakes & Crispybakes		Quick Desserts			
Gluten-free Cooking		Roast			
Grills & Barbecues		Salads			

Photocopy and complete coupon below

Name _____

Address _____

_____ Postcode _____

Country _____ Phone (business hours) _____

Email*(optional) _____

* By including your email address, you consent to receipt of any email regarding this magazine, and other emails which inform you of ACP's other publications, products, services and events, and to promote third party goods and services you may be interested in.

I enclose my cheque/money order for £ _____ or please charge £ _____ to my:

☐ Access ☐ Mastercard ☐ Visa ☐ Diners Club

Card number [| | | | | | | | | | | | | | |]

3 digit security code *(found on reverse of card)* _____

Cardholder's signature _____ Expiry date ____ / ____

To order: Mail or fax – photocopy or complete the order form above, and send your credit card details or cheque payable to: Australian Consolidated Press (UK), 10 Scirocco Close, Moulton Park Office Village, Northampton NN3 6AP, phone (+44) (01) 604 642200, fax (+44) (01) 604 642300, e-mail books@acpuk.com or order online at www.acpuk.com

Non-UK residents: We accept the credit cards listed on the coupon, or cheques, drafts or International Money Orders payable in sterling and drawn on a UK bank. Credit card charges are at the exchange rate current at the time of payment. All pricing current at time of going to press and subject to change/availability.

Postage and packing UK: Add £1.00 per order plus 75p per book.

Postage and packing overseas: Add £2.00 per order plus £1.50 per book.